**The Public Library
of Nashville
and Davidson
County**

Books by Elizabeth Spires

POETRY

Worldling (1995)
Annonciade (1989)
Swan's Island (1985)
Globe (1981)

FOR CHILDREN

With One White Wing (1995)

WORLDLING

Elizabeth Spires

W. W. NORTON & COMPANY
New York   London

The text of this book is composed in Baskerville
with the display set in Herculanum and Baskerville.
Composition by Crane Typesetting Service, Inc.
Manufacturing by The Courier Companies, Inc.
Book design by Charlotte Staub

Library of Congress Cataloging-in-Publication Data

Spires, Elizabeth.
    Worldling / by Elizabeth Spires.
    p.   cm.
    I. Title.
    PS3569.P554W67   1995
    811'.54—dc20   95-7885

ISBN 0-393-03855-6

W. W. Norton & Company, Inc.
500 Fifth Avenue,
New York, N.Y. 10110

W. W. Norton & Company Ltd.
10 Coptic Street,
London WC1A 1PU

1 2 3 4 5 6 7 8 9 0

FOR CELIA DOVELL

If then all that worldlings prize
Be contracted to a rose;
Sweetly there indeed it lies,
But it biteth in the close.

GEORGE HERBERT

CONTENTS

ACKNOWLEDGMENTS

Some of the poems in this book first appeared in the follow-
ing magazines:
The American Voice: "Childhood"
Boulevard: "On the Island"
Image: "Clock"; "The Great Sea"; "Roman Lachry-
matory Bottles"
The Iowa Review: "The Robed Heart"; "The Bodies"
The Kenyon Review: "The Nap"
The New Criterion: "The Awakening"; "The Sum-
mer of Celia"; "Worldling"; "The Unfeminine
Flower"; "Good Friday. Driving Westward";
"The Haiku Master"; "Fisher Beach"; "Life Ever-
lasting"
The New Republic: "Celia Dreaming"
The New Yorker: "Truro"; "Theatre of Pain"; "Easter
Sunday 1955"
The Partisan Review: "The First Day"
Poetry: "Letter in July"
The Southern Review: "The Night and the Doll";
"Two Watchers"
The Southwest Review: "The Rock"; "Mansion
Beach"

"The Haiku Master" also appeared in *The Best American
Poetry 1991*, edited by Mark Strand and series editor David
Lehman (Scribners/Collier, 1991). "Good Friday. Driving
Westward" appeared in *The Best American Poetry 1992*, ed-
ited by Charles Simic (Scribners/Collier, 1992), and in *Walk*

on the Wild Side: Urban American Poetry Since 1975, edited by Nicholas Christopher (Scribners/Collier, 1994). "The Robed Heart" appeared in *The Best American Poetry 1994*, edited by A. R. Ammons (Scribners/Simon & Schuster, 1994). "Letter in July" appeared in *Writing Poems: 4th Edition*, edited by Robert Wallace and Michelle Boisseau (Harper Collins, 1995), and in *Mother Songs*, edited by Susan Gubar, Sandra Gilbert, and Diana O'Hehir (Norton, 1995). "On the Island" appeared in the second edition of *Ecstatic Occasions, Expedient Forms*, edited by David Lehman.

The author would like to thank Gerry Howard for his support and encouragement during the writing of this book and to thank the John Simon Guggenheim Foundation and the National Endowment for the Arts for fellowships which provided time to work on these poems.

I

Men are "the mortals," the only mortal things in existence, because unlike animals they do not exist only as members of a species whose immortal life is guaranteed through procreation. The mortality of men lies in the fact that individual life, with a recognizable life-story from birth to death, rises out of biological life. This individual life is distinguished from all other things by the rectilinear course of its movement, which, so to speak, cuts through the circular movement of biological life. This is mortality: to move along a rectilinear line in a universe where everything, if it moves at all, moves in a cyclical order.

HANNAH ARENDT
The Human Condition

Truro

I found a white stone on the beach
inlaid with a blue-green road I could not follow.
All night I'd slept in fits and starts,
my only memory the in-out, in-out, of the tide.
And then morning. And then a walk,
the white stone beckoning, glinting in the sun.
I felt its calm power as I held it
and wished a wish I cannot tell.
It fit in my hand like a hand gently
holding my hand through a sleepless night.
A stone so like, so unlike,
all the others it could only be mine.

The wordless white stone of my life!

Worldling

In a world of souls, I set out to find them.
They who first must find each other,
be each other's fate.
There, on the open road,
I gazed into each traveler's face.
Is it you? I would ask.
Are you the ones?
No, no, they said, or said nothing at all.

How many cottages did I pass,
each with a mother, a father,
a firstborn, newly swaddled, crying;
or sitting in its little chair,
dipping a fat wooden spoon
into a steaming bowl,
its mother singing it a foolish song,
One, one, a lily's my care . . .

Through seasons I searched,
through years I can't remember,
reading the lichens and stones
as if one were marked
with my name, my face, my form.
By night and day I searched,
never sleeping, not wanting to fail,
not wanting to simply be a *star.*

Finally in a town like any other town,
in a house foursquare and shining,
its door wide open to the moon,
did I find them.

There, at the top of the winding stairs,
asleep in the big bed,
the sheets thrown off, curled
like question marks into each other's arms.

Past memory, I beheld them,
naked, their bodies without flaw.
It is I, I whispered.
I, the nameless one.
And my parents, spent by the dream
of creation, slept on.

Letter in July

My life slows and deepens.
I am thirty-eight, neither here nor there.
It is a morning in July, hot and clear.
Out in the field, a bird repeats its quaternary call,
four notes insisting, *I'm here, I'm here.*
The field is unmowed, summer's wreckage everywhere.
Even this early, all is expectancy.

It is as if I float on a still pond,
drowsing in the bottom of a rowboat,
curled like a leaf into myself.
The water laps at its old wooden sides
as the sun beats down on my body,
a wand, an enchantment, shaping it
into something languid and new.

A year ago, two, I dreamed I held
a mirror to your unborn face and saw you,
in that warped, watery glass, not as a child
but as you will be twenty years from now.
I woke, a light breeze lifting the curtain,
as if touched by a ghost's thin hand,
light filling the room, coming from nowhere.

I know the time, the place of our meeting.
It will be January, the coldest night
of the year. You will be carrying a lantern
as you enter the world crying,
and I cry to hear you cry.
A moment that, even now,
I carry in my body.

The Summer of Celia

Is this a dream? The August sun,
the trees in the moment before their decline,

the high bodiless clouds skimming the horizon,
the water a second skin my strokes

slough off, and Celia swimming
her small strokes inside me as I swim?

Celia, the first and only one,
who fits like a seed in my sleeping palm,

who comes unspeaking to me in dreams,
her eyes half blue, half brown.

I cannot remember my own time, floating
in the warm birth sac, my mother asleep,

the waters still, the two of us dreaming.
What, what did we dream of?

Speak to me, Celia. Speak. Speak.
Before birth erases memory and suddenly

you are taken from me, then given back,
wrapped in the white gown of forgetting,

changed, utterly changed. As I will be.
This is our summer, the summer of the dream

we will, too soon, awaken from,
shocked and surprised, in our separate bodies.

Theatre of Pain

1. 29. 91

In the theatre of pain where all things are born
and brought into the light,
I found myself one night, the world contracting
to a dream of world, a nightmare ocean
I waded into, wave after wave knocking me down,
holding me in pain's undertow until I thought I'd drown.
And then a needle stopped the pain
and I was on an island where no wind blew
and no tree cast a shadow, where to feel nothing at all
was all I could desire. Somewhere a clock ticked madly
but time, for a little while, stood still
until, again, the pain broke through, all flash
and sear, and the moment slowly approached
when we would meet, meet for the first time.
With a final push you were born,
a *fact* engraved upon the world forever, leaving
the two of us half-drowned and clinging to the shore,
hands dragging us back from the black water.
Through corridors of birth and death we were wheeled
to a high room overlooking the city, the rising sun
tinting the clouds, the empty stadium, pink and blue,
rush hour traffic moving soundlessly down 33rd Street,
radios tuned to the morning news,
completely, most completely, unaware of you.
The shift was changing. Breakfast was being brought around.
Two nurses entered with a tray and news of the world
I'd left for a day and returned to, the paper singing
of death, only death, death in the face of life.
How often had they seen that scene before,
the common tableau of mother and sleeping newborn,

your face a perfect rose, so small, so royal?
But no, amazed, they bent over you,
lifting you high into the air,
carrying you with fanfare to the window,
streamers of light everywhere,
saying (I swear to God they said),
"Welcome to the World!"

The Robed Heart

They come in white livery bringing the sun,
the Robed Heart astride her white mount,
crowds lining the royal road in anticipation.
Ahead, the castle flying the new colors,
a queen's great labors come to an end.
A shout, and the cord is cut,
the crown placed upon my head.

And I am, Mother, I am!

The First Day

The ward is quiet, the mothers delivered,
except in one a woman labors still and calls,
with a sharp cry, that she is dying.
She is not dying but cannot know it now.
Trapped in the birthstorm, I did not cry,
but saw my body as the enemy
I could not accommodate, could not deny.
Morning arrived, and my daughter.
That's how it is in this world, birth, death,
matter-of-fact, happening like that.
The room was warm. The room was full of flowers,
her face all petals and leaves, a flower
resembling such as I had never seen.
All day she slept beside me, eyes darting
beneath bruised blue eyelids, retracing the journey,
dreaming the birth dream over and over
until it held no fear for her.
I dared not wake her. The hours passed.
I rested as her soul poured in her body,
the way clear water, poured from a height,
takes the shape of a flaring vase or glass, or light
fills a room's corners on a brilliant winter morning.
Slowly, she opened her eyes, a second waking,
taking me by surprise, a bright being
peering out from behind dark eyes,
as if she already knew what sights would be seen,
what marvels lay ahead of her, weariness and woe,
the joists and beams, the underpinnings of the world
shifting a little to make room for her.
The first day was over forever. Tranced,
I picked up the pen, the paper, and wrote:
I have had a child. Now I must live with death.

Celia Dreaming

Bright sphere, I have watched you dreaming,
your face a wordless whorl, an inward-folding flower
whose petals spiral round a dream of milk and hunger,
a fear of falling farther than outstretched arms
can catch you, while I stand beyond the circle
of your dreaming joy and fear, amazed
that you have been here half a year. Half a year!

Yesterday in the garden as you slept on my shoulder,
I watched a bee tunnel into the Rose of Sharon,
summer's late-blooming flower, watched its head,
then furred legs, disappear completely
into the heart of the flower, back beyond
the body's origin, as if it could be unborn.
Sphere, before you were with me, where were you?

Waking, you reached to touch the white face
of the flower, then another, and another, faces
quickly flowing past us, or held and stared into,
as if between two hands, the way a countenance
that lies in rippling water finally comes clear,
making me wonder how of all the million millions
it is *you*, you who are with me, you and not another.

Childhood

Once, without form or substance, I answered the call,
stepping into the light, into my body.
Only there could I eat and sleep and dream.
Only there could I touch and be touched back,
mouthing the world's words, my voice
                              unspooling inside me.

The season of childhood is summer,
summer's long days, the children at play
on the long lawns wearing their bodies
like shields that dare to reflect the sun.
It was our country for a little while,
we were each, in our time, its first citizen,
and now I turn to look back into it
as one might gaze from a cloud-ridden parapet
                              into a distant kingdom.

I stand among the mothers as they call
their children to *Come in, come in right now.*
How is it that I am here?
When did I change from this to that?
Who changed me? A child, a daughter,
                              answering the call.

There, in the falling dusk, beyond my reach,
she slips in and out of shadow, seeking
the others out, joining a circle of unbroken hands
that lightly dance around the twilit emptiness.
But from each lighted house a mother calls a name,
a child drops out, and night descends, how quickly
                              night descends.

And I hear my voice rise up against the mothers
and what the mothers stand for:
Let the children's game never end.
Let them fall, exhausted, where they stand,
the dew staining their clothes,
the moon on their bodies like a hand.
Let them dream marvellous dreams
as they sleep, immortal, in the long grass.
Let everything remain as it is!

The Awakening

Trying the door,
I bend to enter the playhouse,
too large for the room, the chair,
the rising moon squared in the pane
of the tiny window. The table's set.
My face in the tea plate swims,
like a face set loose from its moorings.
Tonight a crumb will be my portion,
a drop of tea my bitter draught.

Where is she now, the child
who made this house her own dominion?
How easily she has closed the door
on the props of ritual afternoons,
the dolls' lessons and scoldings,
to enter an enchantment of man and beast,
to be the mistress of an immensity
of chilly halls and chambers,
of winding stairs and leaded windows,
each gilded plate, each goblet, held
in her unsure hand, heavy with weight.

She has entered a grave
unchanging kingdom where the restless cries
and footfalls of imagined companions
will not be heard except as whispers
lightly echoing through vast marble rooms,
like drafts from an open window.

Shall I forget this night, this dream?
Forget the wink and tear of the doll

crying at a shard of moonlight in her eye?
Forget the drop of tea that lies
like a stain at the bottom of the teacup?
I wake to the grieving moon-mouth
falling forever over the dark horizon,
wake to the whippoorwill calling her name,
mine, outside the cold casement.
But I have forgotten all in the time
it takes to blink an eye shut and open.

Again the whippoorwill calls.
And again it does.
But the child is gone.
The house stands empty.

The Night and the Doll

Out in the dark yard, the doll looks up at the moon.
Sprawled in the black grass, her dress is stained,
her arms and legs are a jumble.
One fingerless hand lies across her chest,
taking a silent pledge.
The dew is a concentrate, the moment distilled.
She lives for these nights alone, her solitude
a jewel she shows to no one.

She looks and looks at the moon, her gaze unswerving.
How bright it is! How constantly it burns!
How distant! How untouchable!
A great emotion washes over her, like a wave, and passes.
Somebody made her once, but who?
She searches the heavens for a clue
but the heavens don't answer her.
Then she is still, beached on a wordless shore.

Morning comes and the sun.
And the night? The night is forgotten,
like a dreamed pageant that never was.
Out of the doll's half-open mouth comes
a heartbroken sound, like a hiccough.
Just once, she blinks in the too bright light—
so quickly you would not even know—
the animate world flashing and streaming around her.

The Unfeminine Flower

Formally, shall she begin,
greeting her days with ceremony,
bowing to the sun and to the wind.
The air shall be a mirror
she shall not look in, her petals
peaked and stiff as a nun's cowl.
She shall avert her face to the bee's buzz.
Spiked, her stem shall pierce
the Gardener's thick gloves.
In consequence, she shall be passed over.
She shall lose the first flush.

                            Around her,
the rank sweet odor of the garden
in midsummer. And she, untouched.
Parched, she shall not drink,
shall not confess her need. Nor,
knowing her flaw, shall she ask for mercy.
As summer ends, so finally shall she.
Then shall a simple song be sung
by the low and the high choir,
by cricket and fieldmouse and owl,
whose words, if it had words, would be,
She is gone, the proud solitary one . . .
She: the unfeminine flower.

Fisher Beach

Cape Cod

Low tide. Umbrellas dot the beach
in shades of watermelon red, sky blue, and lemon yellow.
The sand bar, completely exposed, lies
like a long spoke poking out into the water.
The bay is warm enough to swim in.
A baby, trailed by its mother, crawls in the shallows,
dipping its nose in, then shaking
its head back and forth violently, like a dog.
The heads of fathers bob in the deeper water;
relaxed, they float on their backs, spout water,
and bellow like sea lions to make their children laugh.
A woman, thin, gray, and frail,
is wheeled onto the beach in a deck chair;
an old sea bird, she flings her head back,
taking long, slow, deep breaths, grateful to simply be here.
The beach is casual, disorderly, adrift
in shifting dunes, blowing paper, and washed-up seaweed,
black, briny, and tangled, like mermaid's hair.
Kites dip in the wind, balls are tossed back and forth,
fortifications go up and come back down again,
everyone doing *something*, if only to lie immobile
on bright towels and, like yesterday's ad
for suntan lotion, brazenly worship the sun.

Yesterday, as the sun went down, we spread
a blanket on the sand bar and ate lobster rolls
to celebrate your birthday, almost come.
It was too windy to light a candle, even one,
but did you remember to wish for something?

Suddenly the light changed, turning grim, gray and wild,
as a storm blew from Boston toward Truro.
The tide reversed itself, the water ice-cold,
but you stripped down for a swim,
your long, slow, sure strokes taking you far out,
your head no bigger than the dot on the letter "i,"
Celia and I retreating, wrapped in a beach towel.
At the horizon, you turned and swam back in,
barely beating the rain, and I let out the breath
I hadn't known I was holding.

Today the light is just right for Sunday painters
or someone more serious, a Seurat or Cezanne
painting promenades and bathers over and over
with everyday titles like "La Plage" or "Sur la Mer,"
hoping to capture life's moment
with a few brushstrokes of color.
Yes, it's easy after a few weeks here
to believe we know this place, to feel it's ours,
but if we drew a picture in the sand and signed our names,
it would all be gone by tomorrow, the way we'll be
when we pack the car at dawn and drive to Baltimore.
Still, three children do just that, raking out
giant letters and hieroglyphs in the sand,
unreadable at ground level but probably legible
from the tiny plane that ferries sightseers all day
back and forth from Provincetown to Buzzard's Bay.
What? What do they say?
Climbing the steepest dune on all fours, a clumsy quadruped,

I can make them out, a few words, a date,
that defy, or underscore, the transience of our stay:

T R U R O   A U G U S T   1

W E   W E R E   H E R E !

On the Island

for Josephine Jacobsen

One ferry arrives as one is pulling out.
July was a high point, hot, bright and buttery.
August is huge and blue, a glittering gemstone
curving dangerously at either end into what precedes
and follows it. The ferry begins as a small white point
on the horizon and gradually enlarges into an event
we don't know whether to dread or impatiently wait for.
Those who have just disembarked look stunned and hopeful.
The trip has been long for them. Down the gangplank
they come, with dogs and bicycles and children,
the sun glaring down, the narrow streets of the town
crowded and loud. Weekends are always busiest.
Up the beach, we who have been here for weeks
are grateful to be going nowhere, to be innocent
bystanders to scenes of greeting and farewell.
We have lived through too many beginnings and ends,
and will again, but not today, thank goodness, not today.
Today we lean back lazily, our chairs set low in the sand,
happy to sit in the safe shadow of a big beach umbrella
and stare out at wide water, our minds emptying
like the plastic watering cans the children use
to wet down the sand. We coexist with them, dreaming
our dreams as they dream theirs, building our castles
in air, in sand, not minding when waves or wind
flood the moats and take down careful curling walls,
calmly rebuilding with the patience of clouds,
the dream we were dreaming beginning all over again.

But there is one among us who does not dream . . .
Waist-deep in rolling water, a woman, a grandmother,

stands in a skirted suit, a bright blue bathing cap
neatly fastened under her chin. Rock-solid, she strides
deeper into the cold blue water, calling back
to her two granddaughters, "Try to keep up with me, girls!"
Out beyond the breakers, she swims rapidly back and forth
between two unmarked points, then rests for a while,
her blue head buoyantly bobbing down and up.
Beaches are big enough for big thoughts that meander
like dogs, sniffing the truth out about themselves.
Will I, too, as I have secretly hoped, give myself up
one day to waves and water, no longer a watcher?
Will I lead the small ones out, fearlessly lead them out,
as if to say, "Courage, dear ones! Beauty will go. Pride, too.
We must take the plunge now or throw in the white towel!"

Like a huge bassoon, the inbound ferry sounds,
shaking the island. To leave here, all must ride it.
Some before others. Some at summer's end and some tomorrow.
Some never to return, and some to come back,
summer after summer, weaving a bright thread of constancy
into inconstant lives. Babies will change
into children, children will awkwardly grow up,
girls will find their slender beauty stolen,
and mothers will wake up grandmothers, they will wake up.
Pursued by change, they will run to the end of their lives,
no other choice left to them, and plunge into
an element darker than sunlight, darker than night.
The ever-widening wake of the inbound ferry
cannot shake the resolve of the woman in the waves.
She follows it out, waving her arms wildly
as she goes, not in distress, oh no,

but simply to give the ones going away a good goodbye.
Soon they will reach the mainland, the summer quickly
becoming a good dream to them, no turning point.
All will go on as it has. Or will it?
They point at the sight of a woman alone in a churning ocean
held up by . . . What holds her up? She waves and waves.
And they, not yet caught up in the life ahead of them,
wave back at her. They wave back.

II

In the age of the world's night, the abyss of the world must be experienced and endured. But for this it is necessary that there be those who reach into the abyss. The turning of the age does not take place by some new god, or the old one renewed, bursting into the world from ambush at some time or other. Where would he return on his return if men had not first prepared an abode for him? How could there ever be for the god an abode fit for a god, if a divine radiance did not first begin to shine in everything that is? The gods who "were once there," "return" only at the "right time"—that is, when there has been a turn among men in the right place in the right way.

What is deadly is not the much discussed atom bomb. . . . What has long been threatening man with death, and indeed with the death of his own nature, is the unconditional character of mere willing in the sense of purposeful self-assertion in everything . . .

MARTIN HEIDEGGER
Poetry, Language, Thought

Clock

In this century more than one hundred million
people have died as a result of war. One rotation
of this hand marks five of those deaths.
The clock was started at 14:40 29 June 1989.
It will reach one hundred million at midnight
on 31 December 1999.

IMPERIAL WAR MUSEUM, LONDON

—The sweep of a hand,
one hand, around the blank white face of the clock.
Black hand on a white face, faster than I can write,
the numbers pulse, rise up and up and up:
963383 . . . 963384 . . . 963385 . . . 963386 . . . 963387 . . .
The dead must be counted, their numbers tallied up,
to rise like ghosts, or stars, into the unimaginable
night of the new millenium, apprehended, dreamed
about for so long it seems the stuff of science fiction.
In my nightmare a hand shadows the turning globe
as lit cities, one by one, fall into darkness
and riotous crowds in the street toast their own oblivion.
The names and faces of our time passing forever out of memory.

*   *   *

Here, in the War Museum, black walls, black ramps
    lead crowds past blown-up, larger-than-life photographs:
a baby in a gas mask, swaddled like a deep-sea diver,
    held up for the camera by its smiling mother;
a group of child evacuees boarding a train,
    some bravely trying to wave, some crying;
and the bodies, row upon row, asleep on the deep platforms
    of the London Underground during the Blitz,

looking for all the world like Christians in the catacombs.
Matter-of-fact horrors juxtaposed with trim generals
    in pressed uniforms pushing pins into maps of the world;
a mustachioed grandfather in the Home Guard, cleaning his rifle
    during teatime, his wife pouring the tea, apparently calm.
WOMEN OF BRITAIN SAY—GO! sings the war poster, as the men
    march off to battle and the wives and children look on.
The silence of these images broken into
    by the wail of a siren, first low and far away,
then building to a high-pitched scream as a bomb
    explodes in a far-off room of the museum.
It's only the newest exhibit, a re-enactment of the Blitz,
    a London street in rubble meant to be
walked through, breathed in, felt in every pore
    as the acrid smell of gasoline and burning rubber
fills the long hall. It's too much for one boy.
    He pulls away from his parents and aims a toy gun
at their heads, screaming, *Bang! Bang! You're dead!*
    and neither his father nor his mother slaps him
to bring him back to the world we're in.
    Nearby, a baby sleeps through it all in a pram.

                *   *   *

Later, outside, the sun slanting across the long lawns
of Harmsworth Park, the day too hot, the parched grass
dying. The same little boy, still firing,
small against the backdrop of artillery and cannon.
Families coming and going, mothers and fathers
buying ice cream from a sidewalk vendor,
frozen confections quickly melting in the children's hands,
only a decade between them and the biggest "party"

the world will ever know, when the century ends with a bang
and we wake, with a start, to the year 2000,
forced to say farewell to a life that will appear,
once gone, quaint and antique in retrospect:
goodbye to typewriters and phonograph records,
to coins and currency stamped with the vanishing profiles
of our time, to books and newspapers, to poetry, goodbye!
The word, once cherished in our lifetime, replaced
by flashing pulses on a screen, by simulations
that can't be held or stilled, the past deleted
by the touch of an unseen hand on a keyboard,
modern memory reduced to an oxymoron. Then will the truth
of these last worst hundred years be revealed?
Or will we lift our eyes upward to the stars
and see no pattern, hear no music of the spheres?
The timeless machinery of the universe moving in perpetuity
but abandoned by an inventor bored, or angry,
with his invention, our reason for being here
collapsing like a star as we find ourselves,
for the first time, alone with what we are.
What are we? Who wants to know?
The words of the boy, gone now, still echo
in my head: *Bang! Bang! You're dead!*
Black hand on a white face, the clock inside
keeps counting, fast as my own heart beats to make me live.
It's 5 p.m. The War Museum is closing its heavy doors,
the crowd, like leaves in the wind, vanishing
in four directions, and I am carried along
to a waiting train, a journey through black tunnels
to a shadowed flat where I, alone, will quickly
turn the light on, waiting for voices, faces

to bring me back. Where are they? Why are they not here?
And then, upstairs, a voice through sleep
calls distantly, "Is it you? Where have you been?"
bright syllables pulling me back from past reverie.
"Yes, yes," I say softly, my foot on the first stair,
"It's me. I'm back. I'm here."

Good Friday.
Driving Westward

. . . being by others hurried every day,
Scarce in a yeare their naturall forme obey:
Pleasure or businesse, so, our Soules admit
For their first mover, and are whirld by it.

JOHN DONNE

The rain. Rain that will not end.
The daily errands. Daily bread.
No letting up. No pause
as I steer blindly, circling
the great city. City of tears and blood.
I woke this morning to the ringing phone.
To the last days of the twentieth century.
Hello. Hello. But the line was dead.
The phone in my hand heavy.
My mind whirling. Numb. Taken
against my will closer to oblivion.
At the mall, a man in rags begging
for a coin. My God, only a coin!
I turned my back. Turned back.
But he was gone. Daily, I turn my back.
The suffering of others more and more
like television. Do I drive East? West?
Do I suffer? Shall anger be divine?
Uncorrected, I steer. Swerve
on a slick patch. Lose control.
The rain letting up now. Clouds torn.
The setting sun a brilliant bloody globe.
As if a nailed hand had violently
raked the sky. And then withdrawn.

Past anger or mercy. Leaving me
more distanced. Alone. Driving
this endless road with all the others.
Night and night's eternity coming on.

Easter Sunday 1955

Why should anything go wrong in our bodies?
Why should we not be all beautiful?
Why should there be decay?—why death?
—and, oh, why, damnation?

ANTHONY TROLLOPE, in a letter

What were we? What have we become?
Light fills the picture, the rising sun,
the three of us advancing, dreamlike,
up the steps of my grandparents' house on Oak Street.
Still young, my mother and father swing me
lightly up the steps, as if I weighed nothing.
From the shadows, my brother and sister watch,
wanting their turn, years away from being born.
Now my aunts and uncles and cousins
gather on the shaded porch of generation,
big enough for everyone. No one has died yet.
No vows have been broken. No words spoken
that can never be taken back, never forgotten.
I have a basket of eggs my mother and I dyed yesterday.
I ask my grandmother to choose one, just one,
and she takes me up—O hold me close!—
her cancer not yet diagnosed. I bury my face
in soft flesh, the soft folds of her Easter dress,
breathing her in, wanting to stay forever where I am.
Her death will be long and slow, she will beg
to be let go, and I will find myself, too quickly,
in the here-and-now moment of my fortieth year.
It's spring again. Easter. Now my daughter steps
into the light, her basket of eggs bright, so bright.
One, choose one, I hear her say, her face upturned

to mine, innocent of outcome. Beautiful child,
how thoughtlessly we enter the world!
How free we are, how bound, put here in love's name
—death's, too—to be happy if we can.

The Rock

For a day and a night
I sat on the rock,
and the sun went down
and the sun came up,

and the tide rushed in
and the tide rushed out,
and I was the center,
the fixed still point.

Behind my back,
row upon row,
the little white houses
were carefully stacked,

one, two, three,
up the hill of stone
that stony forebears
had built the town on.

Did more time pass?
Did a year go by? Two years?
Three? As I held fast
to the rock of my life.

Wind and snow, rain and hail,
the world whirled round me,
whirled my will,
but I was a holdout,

proud by a mile,
who would burn or freeze
before I'd retreat
or drop to my knees.

Before my eyes, the sun
would rise, unblinking eye,
sketching the scene in
with or without me.

Whose will ran the world?
Drew it in its entirety?
But the screaming gulls
wouldn't tell, wouldn't tell.

Finally the cry came,
and the world was words again,
the water, lapping at stones,
cold as a flame is hot.

The cry came. From above
or below? Or was it my own?
Give in, give in, give in.
Give up, give up, give up.

Mansion Beach

1

I count the rays of the jellyfish:
twelve in this one, like a clock to tell time by,
thirteen in the next, time gone awry.

A great wind brought them in, left them here
to die, indifferent time measured by whirling moon
and sun, by tides in perpetual fall and rise.

Englobed, transparent, they litter the beach,
creatureless creatures deprived of speech
who spawn more like themselves before they die.

I peer into each and see a faceless
red center, red spokes like a star.
They are, and are not, like what we are.

2

At noon, in the too bright light, watchful,
looking too hard, we saw the scene turn dark
and lost the children for a moment, waves

crashing around them. Shadow blended with shadow,
the sun inside a cloud, and then the children
were restored to us, our worst fears a hallucination.

All afternoon their castles, poor and proud,
rose and fell. Great civilizations were built,
came to an end, the children mighty lords, their castles

only as small as we are to the stars and starry structures.
The day was infinite for them, time stretching
to the farthest horizon, the sun their overlord.

But how to reconcile these summer days washing away
with our need to commemorate, to hold onto?
They knew. And so they sang a song tuneless and true,

admitting no fixed point, no absolute, words
overheard and blurred by great winds blowing in,
a rhyme or round for a time such as we live in:

The world is made, knocked down, and made again!

3

This is the moment of stasis: gulls stall
above the burned-out mansion on the bluff,
gone for thirty years, and cairns rise up,

stone balanced on stone. By evening, the beach
is empty, my shadow a long-legged giant leading me
past small battlements to the day's masterpiece:

a dripping castle, all towers and crenellation,
tall as a child, made by many children, flying
three-pointed flags that wave hopefully in the wind.

Closer, I see the moat, the courtyard's secret
pool in which, macabrely, red jellyfish float,
death and potentiality entwined forever.

A crab small as my fingernail, dead,
perfect in every detail, with hairlike spinnerets
and claws, guards the open castle door from entry

as night begins to fall and shadows dark as ink
wash in to stain the beach. Shivering, I think,
O sentry, who would enter here?

4

Traveling once, I stood under the open sky
inside a great unfinished cathedral.
Stonemasons, there for generations, clung

like ants to thin scaffolding, carving
griffins and saints, the rising spires and portals
dripping like hot wax, and birds flew

freely in and out of lacy walls, like angels
thrown down from heaven. Gaudy and grand,
it was a vision of eternal mind. Its maker,

dead for a long time, had left no finished plan,
design, but work went on, days turning
into years, the century coming to a close.

In disbelief, I touched each twisting vine
and leaf, marveling at what had been done,
and what was yet to be, and wished,

as I wish now, O let it never be complete!

"Something Happens"
for William Meredith

A man sits beside me at a party,
trying to speak, each word
brought forth after long searching.

> *I want to speak but cannot speak.*
> *I can't say the words.*

Long ago, he wished the wish
all poets wish: to be struck
by lightning. But not like this.

> *I can't read books.*
> *I read the Digest. Terrible!*

Netted like a ghost, his voice
rises off a spinning record our host
puts on. Words spoken years ago:

> *There is a flaw in your design*
> *For you must fall . . .*

He was an airman then, writing
from the other side of the world.
His letters took years to get here.

> *The nodding law has time enough*
> *to wait your fall . . .*

Trapped in the country of no
and yes, he perseveres.
And teaches us how to.

I am getting better.
Something happens.

Poetry provides no rescue.
Yet I'll say these words while I can.
Something is happening to us all.

Seven Gough Square

The old philosopher is still among us in the brown coat
with the metal buttons and the shirt which ought to be
at wash, blinking, puffing, rolling his head, drumming
with his fingers, tearing his meat like a tiger, and
swallowing his tea in oceans.

MACAULAY

"We shall receive no letters in the grave
nor send not even one. You lie, my dear,
in a place of premature tranquillity, and I am left
in an attic room perched on a rickety, three-legged stool
I cannot fix and cannot throw away. Page by page,
I have grown into a great unwieldy tome.
'Dictionary Johnson' I am called, my coat cut
generously to accommodate my words and me.
At the beginning of the World, in Johnson's Bible,
didn't our Maker first create words, then wait,
knowing the proper animal would follow
each name into existence, as love will conjure
a face and form to fix its attentions on?
What does a man, a cat, love? His words, his oysters.
Hodge, licking the oysters in his dish,
exists in a state of sated speechlessness
I envied when your words flew against me.
Tetty, you knew me well enough never to wait for poetry.
Accept now these words, receive my message
in that shadowed place where silence cruelly
predominates. In this dream I am dreaming,
I come to you as I once did, a Nothing and a Nobody
with a proposition, and again we take the great leap,
this time into Eternity. Tetty, it shall not be long.
                    Your husband, Samuel Johnson"

The Haiku Master

Master

Under the plum moon, he sits
like a frog on a lily pad,
waiting, waiting for what?

> *Pupil*
>
> I, too, am illuminated
> by the moon, enraptured
> by the frog's *Thrum! Thrum!*
> My heart beats loudly
> like a big bass drum.

> > *Master/Pupil*
> >
> > He asks with a smile,
> > "What shall you seek, seeker?"
> > And I, the fool, answer,
> > "The stars! The plum moon! Love!"

Pupil

July, August, September . . .
Desire follows desire
these hot sleepless nights
of late summer.

> *Master*
>
> In the mirror: ego.
> The I-maker looks out,
> liking, disliking, what it sees.

Pupil

Great minimalist,
there are too many words!
How shall I choose among them?

Master

Paring the apple, he eats
it slowly, bit by bit.
Down to the nothing of it.

Pupil

October, November, December . . .
Hidden, I watched you
tear the last leaf
from the calendar.

Master

Once, I dreamed the snow
fell all night,
effacing the earth.
And woke to what I dreamed.

Pupil

Once, as the snow fell,
I was at peace
with myself. No more.

Master

Black ink, white paper,
the characters appear:
a farewell party where
I am both host and guest.

Pupil

I saw you to the ferry.
We waved. The pier
I stood on moved away.

Master

Spring. Now I'm a ghost
and you're my dream,
a flame of shadow
in a world of green.

Pupil

You're gone. A cricket
tunelessly sings,
That was a life!

Master

It's black and white here.
I don't care. No koto
plays, but I don't miss it.
Soon I'll be pure spirit.

Pupil

My canvas is ready,
small receding square.
My brush, one hair.
Now to paint what isn't there.

Two Watchers

Dusk. The light on the water contracts to a tear
    where only a minute before
it lay like a long spill, and out of the shadows
    the great blue heron appears
to stand on the periphery of what is and what is not.

Heron, I met you once before on a summer morning
    in the North. You were wading
the shallows of Round Pond when you heard my footsteps.
    Your neck tensed in an "S,"
and then you flew, great wings flapping, toward heaven.

After that, you came to me in a dream, standing over me
    as an angel would, wings unfurled.
Heart to heart, we flew in rushing blackness,
    but I woke too soon, heavy,
without wings. And then you came no more.

As lines cross on a palm, portending joy or sorrow,
    now our lives cross again,
here, in my South, so far from that morning in Maine.
    My heron, why have you come?
Do you dream, as I do, of crossing dark water?

For a moment, we stand here together, two watchers
    watching the night fall.
But the hour approaches when you must fly—fly off!—
    fly through the needle's eye
to save yourself while I must see the winter through,

carrying this moment as lovers do—meeting, parting
how many times over one life, two?—
as the night closes in, and cold cuts to the marrow,
and, distantly, the lights
begin to come on in the great houses of Baltimore.

The Nap

Tragic and intimate
    these lit moments
        passing as we pass . . .

I wake in late afternoon,
    your face floating above me,
        huge, planetary,

gazing deeply into my
    own unguarded eyes. Why
        do these moments terrify?

Agents of cloud, we sleep
    under eaves, under eiderdown,
        and wake to an unfamiliar surround,

an attic room slept in once,
    many times, as dusk is falling.
        A lamp is burning,

framing your face in time's
    aureole, as if the restless moon
        were passing over the sun.

Intolerable, preferred, this solitude
    we bear in which our lives,
        briefly converging,

must swerve, change course, or else
    must merge into an entity
        that is and is not

us: twin bodies held perpetually
    in unbounded space where
        no night, no day, will interfere

with their blind circling.
    We are caught in the present
        and now must rise and live

our lives, the moment gone
    when your face, world weighty
        as my own, eclipsed the room,

took up the sky, laid bare
    the otherness of *I*, and briefly,
        we uncreated the other.

The Bodies

Here, in the half-dark of the sauna,
        the bodies of the women glisten . . .

Naked, disproportionate, lush,
hung and burdened with flesh, they open slowly,
like orchids blooming out of season.

Sweat beads my forehead.
Heat rings my breasts, like circlets,
and I *am* my body, all shimmering flesh.

Secrets are whispered here. Stories told.
The bodies, alabaster, abalone,
relax, give up their pose, to ask,
How shall we be joined?
How shall we know each other?
By doors, by chains and linkages
through which we shall be
        entered, touched, possessed.

I see them, row upon row, the rank and file
of generations moving without pause:
—the bodies of the young girls, the willows,
complete unto themselves, androgynous;
—the great bodies of the mothers,
circled by their little moons, adoring;
—the mothers of the mothers,
the old wise ones, ponderous and slow.
And in another room, not far from this one,
the restless bodies of men, searching
without knowing what it is they search for.

Body of the world! Body of flesh!
Leaving this room, I leave the orbit of women.
I dress and walk into the snowy night,
into the great body of the world,
cold, still, and expectant.
Bodying forth, I am taken by the dark.

What am I? Asked, shall I say:
  Struck by a spark, I quickened
  and was born to flashing
  days and nights, a small significance
  of one. I did not wish to change,
  but changed, feeling desire and fear
  and love, failing many times.
  My meaning made, I died,
  the windows darkening for the last time.

We move, we love, we cry out,
we hold or cannot hold to what we are
and finally wake to find ourselves
changed beyond all imagining.
Was it enough to have lived?
In that moment of still approach,
will it be given to us to know?

The Great Sea

A great sea moves within us, beyond us.
All night I pilot my craft,
the waves unrolling around me
like bolts of black velvet.

A starless night. No moon.
A gull, several gulls, wheeling
overhead, their cries reminding
me of those I have left behind.

But I do not grieve. All
that I need is here: a sail white
as morning, a sheeted bed
I won't sleep in. Not tonight.

On the horizon, a pale glimmering.
I sail toward it, knowing
the sea enfolds and destroys.
But the sea holds.

The wind touches my face.
Or, there is no wind
and I drift, becalmed,
free to forget and remember.

Why am I here? Why?
Why is tonight different
from all other nights?
But the sea makes no reply.

Far off, a voice, many voices
implore, call to me
piteously from the shore:
O where is the great sea?

But I do not answer. I sail on,
over the next wave's hill.
I am alone and complete.
And the journey is everything.

Roman Lachrymatory Bottles

A Vase intended to hold Tears applied by Archeologists
with doubtful correctness to these small phials . . .

THE BRITISH MUSEUM

Of glass, of alabaster, these phials
that held the tears of this one, that one . . .
O who among the dead would hold
tears dear enough to keep forever?

We stand in front of the lit case,
the room bright and hushed, awash
in grief's evaporate, and feel
the need to whisper, as in a church.

Now tears go uncollected, are wept
in secret and run out to sea,
mingling freely with others not of
our making, losing their history.

O let us make a gift to each other:
our stoppered tears, liquid and alive,
poured into jars and bottles
that we drink to the very bottom.

Then we shall be as we once were,
children crying freely, without shame,
then *done* completely, whole again.
Our tears shall wash our faces clean.

There is a liveliness in weeping,
and tears admit no stain, no impediment.
A face shatters, a countenance dissolves,
and wave after wave breaks against the shore.

Our tears rise out of the spray, hang
for a second in grand illumination,
a cherished face, a picture held
in every one of them, and are gone.

Life Everlasting

The sweet earth opened out its wide four corners
to her like the petals of a flower ready to be picked,
and it shimmered with light and possibility till she
was dizzy with it. Her mother's voice, the feel of home,
receded for the moment, and her thoughts turned
forward. Why, she, too, might live forever in this
remarkable world she was only just discovering!
The story of the spring—it might be true!

NATALIE BABBITT
Tuck Everlasting

On a night like any other night, in the house
of our life, foursquare and shining,
I read you the story of life everlasting,
a family in a time before our time,
traveling, where are they traveling to?
Almost before I begin, you want to know
more than I know. The wheels of their wagon
turn as the world turns because the world's
a wheel, too, and then the wheel slows down
and stops in the middle of a summer day
hot enough on a city sidewalk to fry an egg,
except there are no sidewalks here, only
a pathless path leading them, where does it lead to?
As through a telescope, far things seem near,
and near things close enough to touch.
We are, you and I, onlookers to a tale
where the curse will seem, at first, a gift,
impossible to live with, impossible not to,
a mother, a father, and a boy entering
a wood where trees sieve light to shadow,
and creatures stir and live without a thought
to death, the way, too briefly, Adam lived with Eve.

A giant ash presides there, its silver leaves
raised in silent benediction to the air,
while gnarled roots below are splayed
like the fingers of an ancient grasping hand
outspread upon the globe. A spring flows
round the roots, inviting them to drink.
How cold the water looks. How clear.
They drink deep draughts but don't know
what they drink, enchanted water from a world
that lies underneath or side by side the one
we're in, flowing, flowing from Creation's
other side where all things live forever
in a garden rounded on all sides and bounded
by a wall that keeps out death and change.
Yes. Paradise. A plan that failed.
Creepers grow up the outside walls, attracted to
a brightness within that never wavers, never dies.

O waters of life! Eternal flowing waters!
A price must be paid, a reckoning made for endless life!
Expelled from the world of time, our travelers
must wander now in a world where years flow
like a river around them, leaving them untouched.
They stay as they are, never a wrinkle or gray hair,
their clothes a perfect fit but threadbare.
Imagine their life as a line that starts somewhere,
the pencil held by an unseen hand that moves it
round and round the globe without a pause,
the pencil growing dull, the freighted sunrise,
seen for the ten-ten-thousandth time, too much
like yesterday's, tomorrow's, the stars without surprise,
each plate of food the same, the same, the same.

But all stories end in death, even this one,
because the boy falls in love with a girl, mortal
as we are, and gives her all he has to give:
he takes her to the spring and offers her the water.
She kneels, she cups her hands, as if . . .
We are deep in the story, too far in to turn back,
when you stop me with a cry—
                              "Mother, promise never to die!"
And with your words, death enters the picture,
and you refuse it, just as I did when I was five
and begged my mother for the cup, the pill
that would stop all change and keep me
as I was: a child with a store of endless days,
being read to in a bright room, no way
for death to intrude. How little I knew.
I was a child who would have drunk the cup.

But the girl at the spring, what does she choose?
She chooses *change*, a contract with the dead,
and in the moment of her choosing, her childhood
disappears, she sees on the forking path ahead,
leafstrewn and windswept, strangers waiting
for her to catch up: a husband and a child,
her repetition, and beyond, the daughters
of her daughter, mere shadows to her now.
Who are these strangers but the dead come back?
She has made her choice but keeps the water anyway,
tightly stoppered in a vial, hidden away,
only she knows where, to take out and wonder at.
Alone, she sometimes holds it to the light
and sees in the clear suspension that other life,

the one she didn't choose: a bright patchwork
of hill, field, and tree, gone now, to make way
for the town, and a boy tugging at her hand,
the two of them immortal as the sun.
The years pass, each one more quickly, until
she doubts her choice, if she was wise,
her thoughts wound tightly round themselves,
the way a thread is wound around a spool.
The world's too terrible to live in!
I hate the world! she thinks. And goes on.
The world is shadowed and shining. Complete.
And torn. The bright drops in the vial cloud over,
her eyes are cloudy too, as she dies the death
we all die, having completed herself in time.

How late it is. You have fallen asleep,
safe in the words of a story that isn't safe at all.
I close the book, turn the light out, and leave
the door ajar. Tomorrow will you ask me
how the story ended? Or think you dreamed a dream,
strange and unsettling, the way dreams are?
What words complete a tale that ends in death for us all?

The boy returns a lifetime later, believing
he'll find her in the wood, just as she was,
just as he is now. She kept the water, after all.
She might have changed her mind.
He sees her apparition standing by the ash,
holding a hand out to him, warm, *alive*—
                              And touches instead
cold stone, her name freshly engraved, her dates

enclosed in parentheses. No, it's all wrong.
He returns. He is free in a way we cannot imagine.
And perfectly alone. He sees her stone
and wonders again what made her choose against him.
And she, like Eve in death, a spectral presence,
begins to sing, her song rising above the world's
flat hum to move the trees, the stars, and pull him
backward to a wood that isn't there, a spring
where he drank of Time, unknowing, ignorant:
O mortals, do not drink the waters!
All is in flux. All is shining.
The world is spread before you like a table, heavy and laden.
Milk must be poured into mugs and drunk down in great gulps,
and buttered toast heaped onto plates.
The pond is waiting to be rowed on.
The apple tree, with its reaching arms, wants to be climbed.
The fruit on the topmost branch must be taken in hand and eaten.
The swing, so still in the early morning, must be swung on.
The dog must have its stick, its ball, even as the mockingbird
waits in shadow, waits to mock us all. Listen.
The tongues of bells are ringing in the sun
as we climb the bright hill, pause, and go back down.
Each thing is as it does. The world's a wheel.
And death flashes out at us, makes the world shine.

        *   *   *

These are her words. Our only paradise is here,
and we are rich as misers, rich in change!
We hold in our empty hands a currency of days

that we must spend down to the very last,
no holding back allowed. But sleep now.
And I'll sleep, too, to wake with you,
wake to the everlasting present of our life.

A Note about the Author

ELIZABETH SPIRES was born in 1952 in Lancaster, Ohio, and grew up in nearby Circleville. She is the author of three previous collections of poetry, *Globe, Swan's Island,* and *Annonciade,* which received the Sara Teasdale Poetry Award from Wellesley College, and a book of riddles for children, *With One White Wing.* A recent Guggenheim Fellow, she lives in Baltimore with her husband, the novelist Madison Smartt Bell, and their daughter Celia, and teaches at Goucher College and in the Writing Seminars at Johns Hopkins University.